The principal battleground of this war is not the South Pacific.

It is not the Middle East. It is not England, or Norway, or the

Russian Steppes. It is American opinion."

Archibald MacLeish, Director of the Office of Facts and
Figures, forerunner of the Office of War Information

**OWERS OF PERSUASION"** explores the strategies of persuasion as evidenced in the form and content of World War II posters created to galvanize public support for the war.

The National Archives holds approximately 5,000 American World War II posters and some of the original art created for the posters. The holdings include well-known works bearing the signatures of America's most celebrated artists as well as unfamiliar but striking works that remain anonymous. They advocate bond drives, scrap drives, ration plans, and patriotism. They range in mood from the cheerfully patriotic to the grimly resolute. While the majority of the images, to this day, evoke feelings of pride and righteousness, some reveal a less glorious reality driven by prejudice and fear. The collection is a richly varied national resource containing a treasure trove of information about the American homefront during the Second World War.

In commemoration of the 50th anniversary of the United States' participation in World War II, the National Archives presents a sampling of this collection. The posters were products of a government-wide publicity program that had clearly stated goals and strategies. Quotes from government manuals and government leaders provide context, serving as guideposts in a look back at the complicated process of influencing public thought in the midst of the earthshaking global conflict that was World War II.

Guns, tanks, and bombs were the principal weapons of World War II, but there were other, more subtle, forms of warfare as well. Words, posters, and films waged a battle for the hearts and minds of the citizenry just as surely as other weapons fought the enemy. Persuading the American public became a wartime industry, as equally important as manufacturing bullets and planes. The government launched an aggressive propaganda campaign to galvanize public support, and some of the foremost intellectuals, artists, and filmmakers in the nation became warriors on this front. They crafted messages that took the form of pamphlets, posters, and films.

Posters are the primary focus of this publication and exhibition. During World War II, they were ever-present visual reminders of the national war effort. Competing for the attention of the casual observer in a busy visual environment, poster artists composed their works with all the cunning of military strategists. They drew from an arsenal of powerful visual symbols, which were strategically combined with words to evoke a particular response from the viewer—to shape opinion and influence behavior in pursuit of governmental aims.

These images of World War II have stood the test of time. Fifty years after their creation, they continue to capture attention and shape national memories of wartime. The endurance of their designs attests both to the skills of the artists and to the persuasive powers of the federal government.

Contents of the Exhibition and Catalog

The National Archives holds one of the world's largest collections of records relating to World War II. In addition to an extensive collection of printed posters, the National Archives holds some original artwork—sketches, drawings, and paintings—created in the process of poster design and production. The exhibition includes examples of both printed posters and original art.

Some of the artwork shown here bears the original printing instructions, indicating how the art would later be combined with the poster's words. Displayed beside the printed pieces, the artwork reveals a unique vividness and immediacy. Other items appear to have been submitted to the Office of War Information (OWI) for consideration but never became posters; critical comments scribbled in the margins or on the backs offer clues about the standards and priorities of the government poster programs. Still other items seem to be preliminary drawings and sketches presenting various treatments on a particular theme.

This artwork is absolutely unique to the National Archives and presents a rare behind-the-scenes glimpse of American wartime poster production.

Information regarding the posters' dates, artists' names, and originating agencies is provided when it could be determined. Dimensions are given in inches; height precedes width. With the exception of "Buy More War Bonds and Stamps" (page 18), all of the items in this publication are from the holdings of the National Archives. Citations for the posters appear in brackets at the end of each entry.

The exhibition includes more items than are reproduced in this publication; a complete checklist of the exhibition is available through the Exhibits Branch of the National Archives.

Must! Shall!
by James Montgomery Flagg
Watercolor and pencil on thick paper
13 x 9
National Archives, Still Picture Branch [208-AOP-1]

Visual Glossary

Symbols are the vocabulary of poster language. They serve as a visual shorthand for concepts and ideas. Poster designers use them with words and with each other in an infinite variety of combinations to create a powerful, emotionally charged message.

Some of the symbols found in World War II posters are familiar to today's viewers—the Stars and Stripes, the cross, and likenesses of Adolf Hitler; others may be less so. Shown here are some of the symbols that recurrently appear in the posters.

The Continental Congress prescribed the design of a U.S. national flag on June 14, 1777—13 white stars in a blue field and 13 red and white stripes. Since that time, the overall design of the flag has not changed. The **Stars and Stripes** is a symbol of American national pride and unity and appears in numerous World War II posters to evoke feelings of patriotism.

The precise origin of this symbol of the United States is not known. The tall, thin, white-haired, bearded figure evolved from two early American folklore characters, Yankee Doodle and Brother Jonathan. Perhaps the most familiar representation of **Uncle Sam** appeared on James Montgomery Flagg's World War I recruiting poster, which was revived during World War II.

The **Statue of Liberty** is often used as a symbol of the United States. It was a gift from the people of France in celebration of the 100th anniversary of American independence. Sculpted by Frédéric-Auguste Bartholdi, it was placed on Bedloe's Island in New York Harbor as a symbol to arriving immigrants of the freedom and opportunity of America. During World War II, the Statue of Liberty represented the democratic ideals articulated by American leaders to help explain the purpose of the war.

The **swastika** is an ancient symbol used variously to represent the sun, fertility, and good luck. The word *swastika* is derived from the Sanskrit word for well-being. Prior to World War II, factions in Germany and Austria used the swastika as a mark of racial purity and anti-Semitism. The Nazi Party adopted the swastika and chose it to be the national symbol as Adolf Hitler rose to power. Appearing on huge banners, sewn onto uniforms, and printed on posters, the swastika saturated the visual landscape of Nazi Germany. In the United States, it came to represent Nazi aggression. As the war progressed, it eventually came to symbolize evil itself. Since the rise of the Nazi Party, this ancient sign has become inextricably linked to the brutality of the Nazi regime.

The **Rising Sun,** like the images of Japanese leaders, was an easily recognizable representation of the Japanese nation. The rays emanating from the central sphere were removed from the Japanese national flag after World War II.

The **"V For Victory"** was one of the most popular symbols of the war. It was invented by a Belgian refugee who urged resisters in his country to post the symbol in public places as a morale booster. It eventually spread to all the Allied countries. "Vs" became a common motif in war posters and became part of the visual landscape everywhere, affirming the inevitable victory of the Allies.

Service stars were prominently displayed in homes, announcing support and participation in the war. Each blue star on the flag represented a family member in military service; gold stars represented family members who had died in the war.

The **V-Home Award** was a badge of honor presented to households that supported the war in an exemplary way by conserving food, recycling material, buying war bonds, and not spreading rumors.

Skulls and skeletons represent death. Sometimes the skull appears with crossed bones to add intensity to the message. This symbol is used on bottles of medicines and toxic substances as a warning signal. In World War II posters, skulls and skeletons were dressed in Nazi clothing or joined with other Axis-related symbols to suggest the fatal consequences of Axis advances.

The **cross** is one of the most universal and ancient symbols known to mankind. Since the early Christian era, it has been a symbol for the Christian faith. Crosses sometimes appeared in World War II posters to represent the concept of religious freedom; at other times crosses appeared in the form of grave markers, a traditional symbol honoring the death of Christian soldiers.

Fear of **snakes** is nearly universal. Although the snake is a positive symbol for regeneration in the sciences, in other contexts the snake represents a deceitful enemy lurking in hidden places. In World War II posters, snakes symbolize deceit, danger, and death.

Images of World Leaders During the War

During the war, the leaders of the warring nations came to represent the nations themselves. The use of individual images personalized the enemy and focused attention on one person as a symbol of evil or as a symbol of good. The world figures depicted most often in the posters were Franklin D. Roosevelt and Adolf Hitler.

Franklin Delano Roosevelt was the 32d President of the United States (1933–45). A strong leader, he guided the United States through two great crises in American history—the Great Depression and World War II. He died while in office on April 12, 1945, before the end of the war. Since he had been such a popular President and had held the Presidency for so long, invoking his image, especially after his death, rallied the American public.

The Allies viewed **Adolf Hitler** as the instigator of the war and the epitome of all that was evil. Leader of the National Socialist German Worker's Party (Nazi Party) during the 1920s, Hitler became the German Chancellor in 1933 and quickly established a dictatorship and the Third Reich. His control of the German government ended with his suicide in 1945.

PART I

The posters in **Part I** seek to motivate by instilling in the viewer patriotism, confidence, and a positive outlook. Patriotic colors of red, white, and blue predominate. The posters are bright and cheerful, as are the portraits of Americans and their allies. They appeal to our nobler emotions by conveying a sense of national pride to be fighting in a global conflict for what is right.

*T*he exhibition and catalog are divided into two main sections, which represent two psychological approaches used in rallying public support of the war.

Victory Waits on Your Fingers
Photolithograph
22 x 17
Produced by the Royal Typewriter Company for the
  U.S. Civil Service Commission
National Archives, Still Picture Branch [44-PA-2272]

4

These different strategies coexisted throughout the war years. Americans were exposed to both approaches simultaneously. The way in which the posters are presented emphasizes the different techniques used by the government to promote its homefront programs.

It Takes Less Than a Minute For a Man To Die . . .
by Packer
Photolithograph over yellow field
41¼ x 27
Produced by Bressler Editorial Cartoons Company
National Archives, Still Picture Branch [44-PA-1115]

PART II

The posters in **Part II** aim to rock people out of their complacency with grim, unromantic visions of war. They depict the human cost of war, confronting the viewer with corpses, bloodshed, and gravestones. They show peoples who have fallen victim to a brutal enemy and warn that Americans stand next in line. These images appeal to darker impulses, fostering feelings of suspicion, fear, and even hate.

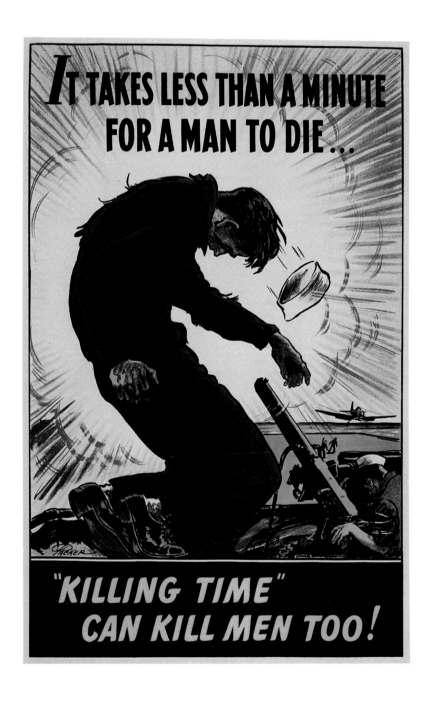

*PROPAGANDA—"The deliberate attempt by the few
to influence the attitudes and behavior of the many
by the manipulation of symbolic communication."*

Terence Qualter, *Opinion Control in the Democracies*, 1985

*"We believe that mass opinion is intelligent and
will support an intelligent program—if informed."*

"Government Information Manual for the Motion Picture Industry,"
Office of War Information

*"The people will put out their fullest effort only if
they are convinced that they are being accurately
informed."*

Elmer Davis, Director of the Office of War Information, to President
Franklin D. Roosevelt, August 4, 1942

*"Posting of official government posters is one of the
most valuable contributions which citizens can
make to the war effort."*

Poster Handbook: A Plan for Displaying Official War Posters,
Office of War Information, 1943

ince American opinion was a crucial element in the formula for victory in World War II, President Franklin Roosevelt created a federal agency, the Office of War Information (OWI), to communicate the war's aims and progress to the American people. Broadcasting and explaining the policies of a burgeoning wartime government was an immensely complicated job and involved government-wide cooperation and coordination.

The OWI developed policies regarding the most important and effective messages to convey to the public. Many OWI campaigns relied on advertising techniques and promotional approaches. To some critics such tactics hinted dangerously of political thought control, which had no place in a free society. President Roosevelt himself resisted the notion of propaganda, even as he saw the need to mobilize public opinion. Political opponents of the President feared that the OWI would serve as Roosevelt's own propaganda agency. Despite this resistance to a centralized government propaganda agency, the OWI disseminated an enormous amount of information to sway public opinion through a monumental effort involving the press, movies, radio programs, and other media.

With regard to posters, the OWI was the primary war poster-producing agency, but it was by no means the only one. Almost every major government agency developed its own posters, as did the armed services and private industry. "Artists for Victory," a nationwide organization of more than 8,000 artists, sponsored national war poster competitions and exhibitions. No single strategy or style prevailed. The fine print at the bottom of the posters in this catalog, crediting a broad range of public and private organizations, documents the multifaceted nature of wartime poster production and may explain why some of the posters actually run counter to specific OWI policies. A multitude of styles appealed both to lofty idealism and to blatant self-interest. There was a cacophony of messages from federal agencies, the armed services, and private organizations—all with their own ideas about how best to enlist public participation in the war effort.

Get Hot—Keep Moving
Screenprint
40 x 28
National Archives, Still Picture Branch [179-WP-1256]

*O*n the back of this print is inscribed: "Bridgeport Brass."

IT'S OUR FIGHT TOO!

"These jobs will have to be glorified as a patriotic war service if American women are to be persuaded to take them and stick to them. Their importance to a nation engaged in total war must be convincingly presented."

Basic Program Plan for Womanpower, Office of War Information, August 1943

In the face of acute wartime labor shortages, women were needed in the defense industries, the civilian service, and even the Armed Forces.

Despite the continuing 20th-century trend of women entering the work force, publicity campaigns were aimed at those women who had never before held jobs. The images glorified and glamorized the roles of working women and suggested that a woman's femininity need not be sacrificed. Whether fulfilling their duty in the home, factory, office, or military, women were shown to be attractive, confident, and resolved to do their part to win the war.

Longing won't bring him back sooner...
GET A WAR JOB!
SEE YOUR U. S. EMPLOYMENT SERVICE
WAR MANPOWER COMMISSION

Longing Won't Bring Him Back Sooner . . . Get a War Job!
by Lawrence Wilbur, 1944
Photolithograph
20 x 14¼
Printed by the Government Printing Office for the War Manpower Commission
National Archives, Still Picture Branch [44-PA-389]

Of all the images of working women during World War II, the image of women in factories predominates. Rosie the Riveter—the strong, competent woman dressed in overalls and bandanna—was introduced as a symbol of patriotic womanhood. The accoutrements of war work—uniforms, tools, and lunch pails—were incorporated into the revised image of the feminine ideal.

We Can Do It!
by J. Howard Miller
Photolithograph
22 x 17
Produced by Westinghouse for the War Production
   Co-Ordinating Committee
National Archives, Still Picture Branch [179-WP-1563]

It's Our Fight Too!
by Jack Campbell
Photolithograph
22 x 17
Produced by the Douglas Aircraft Company
National Archives, Still Picture Branch [179-WP-1565]

HELP BRING THEM BACK TO YOU!

"This is a colossal sweepstakes in which Mr. Civilian has everything to lose and everything to win. The price of a ticket on the winning side is a mere matter of getting along on less for the duration and working harder."

"Government Information Manual for the Motion Picture Industry," Office of War Information

On the homefront, the government needed civilians to perform a variety of war-related tasks. Mobilization campaigns addressed civilians as soldiers on the homefront whose behavior at home had military consequences overseas. Posters visually reinforced this relationship and reminded people that every aspect of life presented an opportunity to support the war.

Help Bring Them Back To You!
by Francis Criss, 1943
Photolithograph
28 x 22
Printed by the Government Printing Office
    for the Office of War Information
National Archives, Still Picture Branch [44-PA-951]

The slogans on this poster touched on nearly every major homefront campaign aimed at involving citizens in the war effort. Its visual elements, the service flag and window card, were common sights during World War II, when families proudly displayed them as public symbols of their contributions to the war effort.

HELP BRING THEM BACK TO YOU!

Find time for war work

Raise and share food

Walk and carry packages

Conserve everything you have

Save 10% in War Bonds

THIS IS A V HOME

MAKE YOURS A VICTORY HOME!

You Make It Right . . . They'll Make It Fight
by Bernard Perlin, 1942
Photolithograph
40 x 28 ½
Printed by the Government Printing Office for the War Production Board
National Archives, Still Picture Branch [44-PA-2504]

*I*n this graphic, executed in red, white, and blue, the soldier and factory worker merge as each performs his patriotic duty.

USE IT UP, WEAR IT OUT, MAKE IT DO, OR DO WITHOUT

Popular saying, ca. 1943

"Astronomical quantities of everything and to hell with civilian needs."

Donald Nelson, Chairman of the War Production Board,
describing the military view of American wartime industry

Although the United States did not suffer the same kind of war deprivations that Europe did, there were wartime shortages. Gasoline, rubber, sugar, butter, and meat were among the rationed items. Government publicity reminded people that the shortages occurred because the materials were going to the troops and that civilians should take part in conservation and salvage campaigns.

Posters exhorting people to conserve used upbeat messages emphasizing fairness in distribution. They are inhabited with patriotic, civic-minded people who good-naturedly adapt to the conservation measures necessitated by the war.

Waste Helps the Enemy
by Vanderlaan
Photolithograph
22 x 17
Produced by the Douglas Aircraft Company
National Archives, Still Picture Branch [179-WP-103]

Many posters relating to food rationing combine contradictory elements: Images of abundance accompany words warning of shortages.

Can All You Can
1943
Photolithograph
22½ x 16
Printed by the Government Printing Office
for the Office of War Information
National Archives, Still Picture Branch [208-PMP-77]

Wastin' That "Solid Rubber" Ain't In The Groove
Silkscreen
20 x 13½
Produced by the Emerson Electric Manufacturing Company
National Archives, Still Picture Branch [179-WP-81]

**Save Waste Fats for Explosives—
Take Them to Your Meat Dealer**
by Henry Koerner, 1943
Photolithograph
28 x 20
Printed by the Government Printing Office
   for the Office of War Information
National Archives, Still Picture Branch [44-PA-380]

STAMP 'EM OUT!

"War posters that are symbolic do not attract a great deal of attention, and they fail to arouse enthusiasm. Often, they are misunderstood by those who see them."

How to Make Posters That Will Help Win The War,
Office of Facts and Figures, 1942

The government tried to identify the most effective poster style. One government-commissioned study concluded that the best posters were those that made a direct, emotional appeal and presented realistic pictures in photographic detail. The study found that symbolic or humorous posters attracted less attention, made a less favorable impression, and did not inspire enthusiasm. Nevertheless, many symbolic and humorous posters were judged to be outstanding in national poster competitions during the war.

Many of the symbolic posters depict American muscle smashing, cracking, or crushing swastikas, rising suns, and likenesses of Hitler.

More Production
by Zudor
Photolithograph
40 x 28 ½
Printed by the Government Printing Office
  for the War Production Board
National Archives, Still Picture Branch [208-PMP-129]

Buy More War Bonds and Stamps
Photolithograph
34 x 24
Produced by R. Hoe & Co., Inc.

Courtesy Prints and Photographs Division, Library of Congress

Stamp 'Em Out!
Photolithograph
30 1/2 x 21 1/2
Produced by RCA Manufacturing Company, Inc.
National Archives, Still Picture Branch [44-PA-1795]

"Commercial advertising usually takes the positive note in normal times. . . . But these are not normal times; this is not even a normal war; it's hell's ideal of human catastrophy [sic], so menace and fear motives are a definite part of publicity programs, including the visual."

"Statement on Current Information Objectives," Office of Facts and Figures

The posters in this section take a radically different approach. They do not accentuate the positive. They are filled with images of dead bodies, wounded soldiers, and monstrous enemies. With emotionally powerful images, they show America and its allies at risk.

The strategy of these posters was to energize the public—not with the justness of the Allied cause but with the enormity of the Nazi and Japanese threat. While posters from the first part of the exhibition and catalog are relentlessly upbeat, these posters hint at a grimmer reality of war. Poster artists did not go so far as to portray war in all of its gruesomeness; even images of corpses were sanitized and romanticized for public consumption. Nevertheless, in highly stylized compositions, these posters acknowledged the inevitable human cost of war and warned Americans about the consequences of defeat.

Miles of Hell to Tokyo
by Amos Sewell, 1945
Photolithograph
26 x 18 ½
Printed by the Government Printing Office for the War Manpower Commission
National Archives, Civil Reference Branch [211-E195-Box 2]

Have You Really Tried To Save Gas By Getting Into a Car Club?
by Harold Von Schmidt, 1944
Photolithograph
40 x 28 ½
Printed by the Government Printing Office
National Archives, Still Picture Branch [200(S)-PSC-16]

Many posters promoting conservation of war-related materials delivered a strong dose of guilt along with messages about the need to conserve.

HE'S WATCHING YOU

"Words are ammunition. Each word an American utters either helps or hurts the war effort. He must stop rumors. He must challenge the cynic and the appeaser. He must not speak recklessly. He must remember that the enemy is listening."

"Government Information Manual for the Motion Picture Industry," Office of War Information

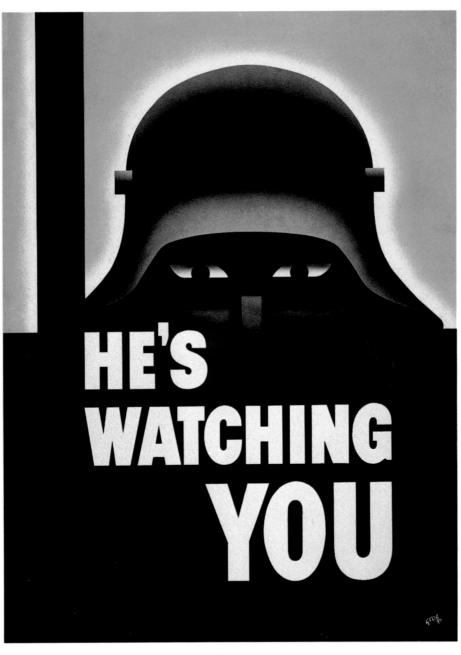

Concerns about national security naturally intensify during war. During World War II, the government alerted citizens to the presence of enemy spies and saboteurs lurking just below the surface of American society. In a campaign that seemed to encourage a mild paranoia, "careless talk" posters warned people that small snippets of information regarding troop movements or other logistical details could be useful to the enemy. Well-meaning citizens could easily compromise national security and soldiers' safety with careless talk.

Art for **He's Watching You**
by Glenn Grohe, ca. 1942
Gouache on cardboard
40 ¾ x 30 ¾
National Archives, Still Picture Branch [208-AOP-119]

Award for Careless Talk
by Stevan Dohanos, 1944
Photolithograph
26 x 20
Printed by the Government Printing Office
   for the Office of War Information
National Archives, Still Picture Branch [44-PA-156]

A sophisticated design, this poster employed symbols of Nazi Germany rather than graphic pictures of death to convey its message of careless talk. It became one of the best known posters on this theme.

A woman—someone who could resemble the viewer's neighbor, sister, wife, or daughter—was shown on a "wanted" poster as an unwitting murderess. The viewer was to conclude that this woman's careless talk resulted in the death of American soldiers.

At least one viewer voiced objection to the choice of a female model. A letter from a resident of Hawaii to the Office of War Information reads, in part, "American women who are knitting, rolling bandages, working long hours at war jobs and then carrying on with 'women's work' at home—in short, taking over the countless drab duties to which no salary and no glory are attached, resent these unwarranted and presumptious [sic] accusations which have no basis in fact, but from the time-worn gags of newspaper funny men."

Wanted! For Murder
by Victor Keppler, 1944
Photolithograph
28 x 20
National Archives, Still Picture Branch [208-PMP-91]

WARNING! OUR HOMES ARE IN DANGER NOW!

"Civilians must have the war brought home to them. Every individual must be made to see the immediacy of the danger to him. . . . He must be made to understand that he is an integral part of the war front, and that if he loses the war, he loses everything."

"Government Information Manual for the Motion Picture Industry," Office of War Information

Poster makers used fear to mobilize the public. In the absence of any immediate physical danger, American propagandists exaggerated the physical proximity of the enemy forces. Though separated from the actual warfare by great distances, Americans appeared within arm's reach of the enemy. They were shown to be in imminent danger—their backs against the wall and living in the shadow of Axis domination.

WARNING! Our Homes Are In Danger Now!
1942
Photolithograph
40 ¼ x 30
Produced by the General Motors Corporation
National Archives, Still Picture Branch [44-PA-2314]